Blast
to the Moon!

Written by Michaela Morgan

Collins

We have always looked up
at the Moon and wanted
to get there.

First, we had to go up into space, but things kept going wrong.

At last we sent a **rocket** into space. It had a **satellite** on it.

the satellite in space

This dog went into space.

Next we sent animals into space.

After that, we sent the first man and the first woman into space.

the first woman in space

the first man in space

Space travellers are called **astronauts**.

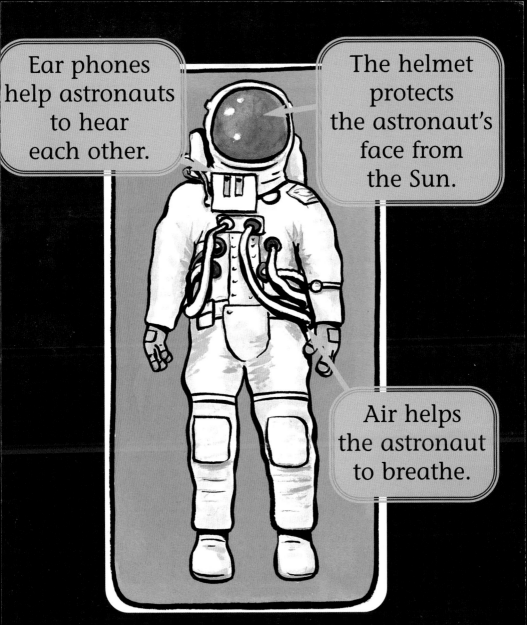

Astronauts have to wear a **spacesuit**.

In space everything seems to float.

Astronauts eat special food
and drink from special cups.
They don't want their dinner
to float away.

At last astronauts landed on the Moon and began to explore.

This man walked on the Moon.

There is no wind on the Moon, so their footprints are still there.

footprint

Going to the Moon

satellite i[r]

firs[t]
t[h]

Glossary

astronauts: people who go into space

rocket: a long, pointed tube that flies up into space

satellite: an object that flies around the Earth

spacesuit: special clothes worn by astronauts

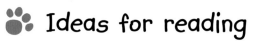 Ideas for reading

Written by Clare Dowdall, PhD
Lecturer and Primary Literacy Consultant

Reading objectives:
- discuss the significance of the title and events
- make inferences on the basis of what is being said and done
- explain clearly their understanding of what is read to them

Spoken language objectives:
- give well-structured descriptions, explanations and narratives
- use relevant strategies to build their vocabulary
- use spoken language to develop understanding through speculating and exploring ideas
- ask relevant questions to extend their understanding and knowledge

- maintain attention and participate actively in collaborative conversations

Curriculum links: ICT

High frequency words: we, have, up, at, the, and, to, there, first, had, go, but, last, a, it, no, one, in, it, next, this, dog, after, that, man, are, called, help, from, they, want, their, away, last, on, is, so

Interest words: spaceship, protects, astronauts, space, travellers, spacesuit, satellite

Word count: 185

Resources: whiteboard, ICT, junk modelling

Build a context for reading

- Read the title and the blub. Focus on tricky words and demonstrate a range of decoding strategies, e.g. illustrations, context.
- As a group, discuss what it might be like on the Moon. Use questions to develop children's language and understanding.
- Create a list of questions on the whiteboard that children would like to ask an astronaut.

Understand and apply reading strategies

- Read pp2–3, look at the pictures and ask what is happening, providing vocabulary if necessary, e.g. *telescope*.
- Ask children to read pp4–13 in pairs. Remind children of the strategies that can be used for reading new and tricky words.